HABITAT
VANCOUVER 1976

UNITED NATIONS
CONFERENCE
ON HUMAN
SETTLEMENTS

AN OUTLINE
OF PLANNING
IN THE
UNITED
KINGDOM

DEPARTMENT OF THE ENVIRONMENT

LONDON HER MAJESTY'S STATIONERY OFFICE

CONTENTS

2

This book is a shortened version of the full United Kingdom
National Report to the 1976 United Nations Conference on
Human Settlements Habitat.

This map has been compiled to show the physical features of Britain and the main centres of population. The numbered shaded areas are the conurbations (1 Central Clydeside, 2 Tyneside, 3 West Yorkshire, 4 South-east Lancashire, 5 Merseyside, 6 West Midlands, 7 Greater London), which are the largest concentrations of urbanisation and which in some cases straddle local authority boundaries.

Inverness

Aberdeen

SCOTLAND

Perth
Dundee

Dunfermline

Atlantic Ocean

1
Glasgow
EDINBURGH

Ayr

Newcastle
2
Carlisle
Sunderland

Londonderry
**NORTHERN
IRELAND**
BELFAST

Middlesbrough

North Sea

Irish Sea

York
3 Leeds Hull
Preston
4 Bradford
Liverpool Sheffield Grimsby
5
Manchester Lincoln
Chester

Stoke
on Trent Nottingham
Derby Peterborough
Shrewsbury Leicester Norwich
Wolverhampton 6 Birmingham
Coventry
Northampton Cambridge Ipswich
WALES Hereford **ENGLAND**
Luton
Gloucester Oxford
Swansea Swindon 7
CARDIFF Bristol Reading LONDON

Exeter Bournemouth Southampton Portsmouth Brighton

English Channel

Plymouth

50   10
0   50   100   150

4

INTRODUCTION

A world problem
The United Nations 1972 Stockholm conference concentrated on safeguarding man's natural environment. Habitat Vancouver 1976 is about human settlements – man's habitat in city, town and village. Faced with the prospect of an additional 3,500 million people to be fed, clothed and housed by the year 2000, the world's governments face immense difficulties. Yet human settlements are more than houses. They demand jobs to match homes; schools, hospitals, shops, social services; and recreational provision.

Britain's experience
The United Kingdom national report* looks critically at how Britain has tried to deal with these problems over the years. Britain does not claim to know all the answers. We have too many unsolved problems of our own to be other than modest. But Britain was the first country to have to cope with industrialisation. So our experience may at least provide a guide to some of the pitfalls as well as a source of positive ideas.

Component parts of the United Kingdom
The United Kingdom has different planning systems and laws for England and Wales, Scotland, and Northern Ireland. In this book we use "Britain" to mean "United Kingdom"; reference is primarily to law and practice in England and Wales; but footnotes indicate some of the more important differences in Scotland and Northern Ireland.

*Planning in the United Kingdom, Habitat Vancouver 1976, Department of the Environment 1976, £10.

Town planning in the early decades of this century is epitomised by Welwyn Garden City, Hertfordshire, established in 1920. The spacious roads, the detached houses and the preservation of a country air were a positive reaction against the cramped and ugly developments of the early industrial towns.

PART 1 THE EARLY STAGES OF PLANNING

Leeds, West Yorkshire, in the 18th century and (below) 100 years later. The contrast illustrates dramatically the physical impact of the industrial revolution.

In its early stages there were no restrictions on the siting of factories near houses, or even on the dumping of industrial waste in town or countryside.

THE EARLY STAGES OF PLANNING
1 SETTING THE SCENE

A pioneer's penalties

Many of the United Kingdom's present planning problems result directly from the rapid urban development of the 19th century, which was earlier and faster than in any other country. Already by 1900 60 per cent of its 38 million population lived in towns. That century's experience shows all too clearly how development can turn sour when no real attempt is made to plan in the interests of the community as a whole.

Industrial revolution

Britain in the late 18th century was still predominantly an agricultural country. In a total population of 11 million, only two cities, London and Edinburgh, had more than 50,000 people. Then came the industrial revolution, and with it the rapid growth of new industrial areas close to water-power, coal and iron deposits and shipbuilding rivers. Politically this was a period of laissez-faire. No one questioned the industrialist's right to dump his rubbish in great tips that spoiled both countryside and town.

Some industrialists came to realise that the workers' living conditions could no longer be tolerated. In *1799 Robert Owen, a cotton manufacturer, bought a mill at New Lanark, near Glasgow, and built a complete* *"model" community, including living accommodation, a school (lower picture), food shops and a market.*

Industrial growth
brought great prosperity
to some, and elegant
streets and buildings,
often in the classical
style, appeared in many
towns. (Top) An
18th-century residential
street in Edinburgh.
(Above) Waterloo
Place and Lower Regent
Street, London – the
southern end of John
Nash's Regent Street
project of 1825.

11

Urban squalor

Fast-growing industry drew in agricultural workers in their thousands, while the population grew from 11 million in 1800 to 38 million in 1900. They found homes in terrace upon terrace of tiny houses, ill built, crowded together, often back to back[1]. Water and sanitation failed in many places to cope; the new urban areas lacked social services or parks for children to play in, and homes were typically dominated by factory and slag-heap.

In spite of the new prosperity, the overwhelming picture of this period was of industrial squalor, with hundreds of homes constantly under a pall of smoke from nearby factories. This is Sheffield, South Yorkshire, in the early 19th century.

First reforms

But some reforms did occur. Workers' self-help produced "friendly societies" (precursors of the trade unions) and consumer co-operative societies: and a few employers like Robert Owen[2] showed that providing better housing and social facilities need not damage profits. Social conscience and fear of disease moved Parliament to legislate to improve urban conditions. The 1875 Public Health Act, which gave local authorities power to control the layout and construction of streets and buildings, ranks as a first step in modern town planning legislation. In 1890, Parliament also gave the local authorities powers to demolish slums and build new artisan housing at public expense.

A mixed legacy

Nineteenth-century Britain offers some examples of well-planned new towns and districts, such as Nash's[3] Regent's Park terraces in London, much of Edinburgh's New Town and the squares and crescents of Brighton. But the overwhelming picture is of industrial squalor.

1. Back-to-back houses consisted of two terraces backing onto each other, thus receiving light and ventilation from one side only.
2. Robert Owen (1771–1858), early Socialist and founder of the Co-operative Movement.
3. John Nash (1752–1835) architect-planner who laid out Regent's Park, London, and designed many of the surrounding terraces.

2 BEGINNINGS OF MODERN PLANNING

Overcrowded slums

Britain entered the 20th century with 38 million people, almost four times the 1800 population. London had 4.5 million, but the industrial north and Midlands and parts of Scotland and Wales showed the worst conditions, with most working people living in houses hastily and shoddily built, overcrowded, and in a drab and unhealthy environment. High birth rates and reduced infant mortality, due to medical advances, aggravated overcrowding.

Garden cities

Gradually public opinion accepted that only town planning could prevent such conditions. Ebenezer Howard's first "garden city" at Letchworth (1903) demonstrated that working people could have good homes in attractive surroundings; and legislation permitted local authorities to make plans controlling new housing, though their powers were totally inadequate. That year Liverpool University started a civic design department; and in 1914 the Town Planning Institute was founded. Planning as a serious professional activity had arrived.

Post-war housing drive

After the 1914–18 war, the Government made "Homes for Heroes" its priority and provided subsidies. This produced many large municipal housing estates, their houses well built and spacious, to densities of 30 persons to the hectare and with generous gardens. But they were monotonous and drab and often lacked shops, pubs, churches and all other amenities. Their failings strengthened the Garden City Movement's plea for self-contained new towns. In inner city districts, councils cleared 18th- and 19th-century slums, replacing them with 4- and 5-storey "walk-up" flats.

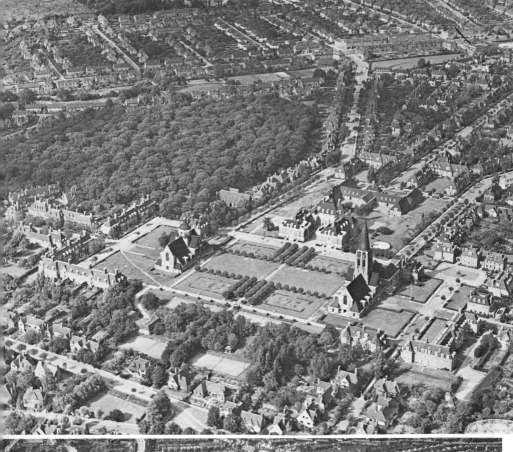

Unplanned growth

Alongside municipal housing, the private house market grew rapidly, making possible owner-occupation even by people of modest means. Hampstead Garden Suburb (started 1905) and Welwyn Garden City (1920) set high design standards; but expanding public transport and plentiful mortgage finance triggered off a rash of speculative development often to lower standards than the municipal estates. While in theory local councils had power to plan future land uses, this entailed compensation for loss of profitable uses, which provided a formidable deterrent for most councils. Moreover, all but the largest local authorities lacked resources and expertise to invoke the Act.

Green belts, commuters and industrial location

The 1930s did, however, see Britain's first attempts to control the sprawl of cities. In 1938 the London County Council (LCC) took powers to establish a "green belt" round London (see also Chapter 11); in 1935 legislation was introduced to curb the undesirable "ribbonning" of houses along main roads. Industry and commerce, however, concentrated increasingly on city centre sites, producing traffic congestion. Public transport – first trams, then buses, electrified suburban railways and, in London, the much extended Underground system – encouraged commuting from greater and greater distances. The inter-war period (1919 – 1939) also saw the first tentative steps towards regional economic planning. (See Chapter 7.)

3 A NEW START AFTER THE 1939-45 WAR

Three crucial reports

Virtually no urban development took place during the 1939-45
war, but planning for the peace began in the darkest days of 1940.
Lord Reith, as minister responsible, had to hand three vital
reports: Barlow on industrial location; Uthwatt on "compensation
and betterment"; and Scott on rural land utilisation. In 1943, the
Government set up a separate Ministry of Town and Country
Planning under a minister charged with securing consistency and
continuity in land use and development in England and Wales [1].
From the Barlow Report sprang Britain's post-war regional
planning policies (Chapter 7) and the new towns (Chapter 4).
Another dominant preoccupation, the post-war housing crisis, is
discussed in Chapter 8.

A new planning system

The 1947 Town and Country Planning Act formed the keystone
to the post-war planning system and provided the statutory basis
for the next two decades' land-use planning. Broadly, all
"development" [2] became subject to consent from the local
planning authority [3]; and each authority was to draw up a
"development plan" as a broad policy yardstick against which to
decide individual applications. These plans, comprising both
explanatory policy statements and programme maps of the
development expected over the next two decades, were based on
thorough land-use surveys and analysis of foreseeable change.
They needed ministerial approval, given only after a public
inquiry which gave objectors a chance to argue against specific

proposals. The Act reduced the number of planning authorities from 1,441 to 145 (counties and large towns only); and also gave them power to preserve trees, control outdoor advertising, and protect buildings of special architectural or historic interest. (See Chapter 11.)

System's strengths and weaknesses

The system, despite its great strengths and achievements, had several major weaknesses: plan preparation, approval and review took too long; the system could not respond quickly enough to changing conditions and public values; it treated the physical land-use system in isolation and paid too little heed to economic and social factors; and it failed to integrate land-use and transport adequately.

Development and land values

The 1947 Act also implemented the Uthwatt Committee's main recommendation that increased land values attributable to development should accrue to the community, not to the individual owner. Owners were to pay a development charge – fixed initially at 100 per cent of development value – when the development was carried out [4]. (See also Chapters 6 and 10.) In 1953 a Conservative government abolished these charges on the grounds that they deterred desirable development; but the principle had been established that refusal of planning permission gave no right to compensation. Planning authorities, freed from fear of heavy compensation bills, have been able to allocate land to better advantage and preserve open country and good farmland from development. The post-war period also saw the strengthening and extension of green belts round cities; the establishment of national parks; and other measures to conserve and give access to attractive countryside. (See Chapter 11.)

Notes
1. A separate Act gave the Secretary of State for Scotland similar functions in that country.
2. "Development" means "the carrying out of building, engineering, mining or other operations in, on or under the land, or the making of any material change of the use of any building or other land". The "general development order", however, exempts certain kinds of development from the need for planning permission, including, for instance, minor extensions to dwelling houses.
3. The local planning authority is responsible for the administration of planning control.
4. Where an owner could show that his land had established its development value before the introduction of the new system, he was eligible for compensation.

THE EARLY STAGES OF PLANNING

4

NEW TOWNS

The post-war policy

Britain's new towns, undoubtedly one of the success stories of post-war planning, stemmed directly from the Barlow Committee's recommendations for dispersal of population and employment. The initial strategy prescribed dispersal from London's congested inner areas, leap-frogging the existing suburbs and the green belt, to an outer ring some 50–60 km from the centre.

The 1946 New Towns Act empowered the minister to designate land for a new town after consulting local authorities and statutory boards providing such services as water, electricity and drainage. After a procedure which normally includes a public inquiry, he appoints a "development corporation" – quite separate from the elected local authorities – which buys the land, prepares plans, builds houses and initiates other development. Central government exercises planning powers and provides much of the finance.

Facing the problems

The planners of new towns encountered many problems. Finding suitable sites was not easy. Then development corporations needed to provide shops and services for early residents; persuade industry to move in so that jobs could be matched to homes; and cope with imbalance in the migrating populations, whose dominant age groups were 20–30 and 0–5 years. By 1960 the first 15 new towns had provided more than 100,000 new homes. Britain's new towns demonstrate that careful and imaginative planning can create good living conditions and a better overall environment[1].

Typically, a post-war British new town, aiming at an ultimate population of 60,000–100,000, consists of a series of village-like neighbourhoods grouped round the town centre. Each has a primary school, community hall, clinic, local shops and pub within easy walking distance of all houses; the road pattern

1. The 1960s also saw the designation of four new towns in Northern Ireland.

New towns and Town Development Act expansions.

1 Glenrothes
2 Cumbernauld
3 Livingston
4 East Kilbride
5 Stonehouse
6 Irvine
7 Londonderry
8 Ballymena
9 Antrim
10 Craigavon
11 Washington

12 Peterlee
13 Aycliffe
14 Central Lancashire
15 Skelmersdale
16 Warrington
17 Runcorn
18 Telford
19 Peterborough
20 Corby
21 Redditch
22 Northampton

23 Milton Keynes
24 Stevenage
25 **Welwyn Garden City**
26 Harlow
27 Hemel Hempstead
28 Hatfield
29 Basildon
30 Bracknell
31 Crawley
32 Newtown
33 Cwmbran

□ New towns

✳ Town expansions (schemes of less than 5,000 households not shown)

⬛ Conurbations

The new towns and town
expansions attempted to
give their housing the
best that had been
learned from the garden
cities. (Left) A
residential road in
Welwyn Garden City
and (below left)
housing at Harlow New
Town. The new towns
also offered wide scope
for the application of the
latest ideas in town
planning and
architecture, including
pedestrian shopping
precincts and the
segregation of local and
through traffic. (Right)
The town centres at
Hemel Hempstead
(top) and Harlow
(lower two pictures).

Town expansion scheme at Thamesdown, Swindon, Wiltshire: (left) traffic-free shopping centre; (below left) safe access to housing through pedestrian pathways. (Right) Aerial view of Cumbernauld New Town, looking north with the town centre on the left, showing how the road system has been planned to provide direct access to the residential areas.

excludes through traffic; and there are separate road and footpath (sometimes also cycleway) systems. Most houses are built for rent though successive governments have sought to increase owner-occupation.

Diversity and experiment

But there is much diversity, made possible by government's policy of leaving development corporations to make their own decisions within broad national guidelines. For instance, Cumbernauld in Scotland pioneered a more compact, higher-density town built round a multi-level shopping centre set above a high-capacity road system. Runcorn, on Merseyside, has been planned round a reserved-track busway which gives public transport a built-in advantage over the private car.

Town expansion schemes

In 1952 legislation provided a means of supplementing the new towns' contribution to urban dispersal. It allowed overcrowded conurbations to make agreements, usually with small towns, under which they jointly built houses and factories to expand those towns. Central government gave financial help, and the Act

The latest new towns have been planned from the start to take full account of social and conservation needs. (Left) Milton Keynes, Buckinghamshire, will eventually have a population of 250,000. As it grows, the town is being designed to blend in with existing settlements, such as the village seen beyond the ring road, and with the countryside, which is being preserved as far as possible. (Below) Children's play area, safely away from roads, at Runcorn New Town.

enabled the partner authorities to buy land cheaply; but the local authorities retained responsibility and control. The LCC and its successor the Greater London Council (GLC) have been the major initiators, with more than 100,000 houses built or planned in 36 expanding towns, some of which are hard to distinguish in appearance from those built under the New Towns Acts.

The later new towns

The latest generation of new towns proper aim at very much larger ultimate populations than previously – 180,000–420,000 – and mostly also base themselves on the expansion of substantial existing settlements – Peterborough (1967), Northampton (1968), Warrington (1968) – in partnership with local authorities. One, however, Milton Keynes (1967), already shows the benefits to be gained on a green-field site when physical planning is geared firmly to the needs of social planning (see also Chapter 10). For instance, health services are to be community-orientated: health centres catering for some 30,000 people each will provide both bases for family doctor teams and much of the specialist out-patient treatment normally found only in hospitals.

Many features that
foreshadow the latest
thinking on town
planning and design –
the emphasis on the total
environment, including
social factors; the
importance of the
human scale in
developments; the
conservation and
rehabilitation of
existing buildings – are
to be seen in Coventry,
which suffered
extensive war damage
and now provides one of
the best examples of
comprehensive city
centre redevelopment.

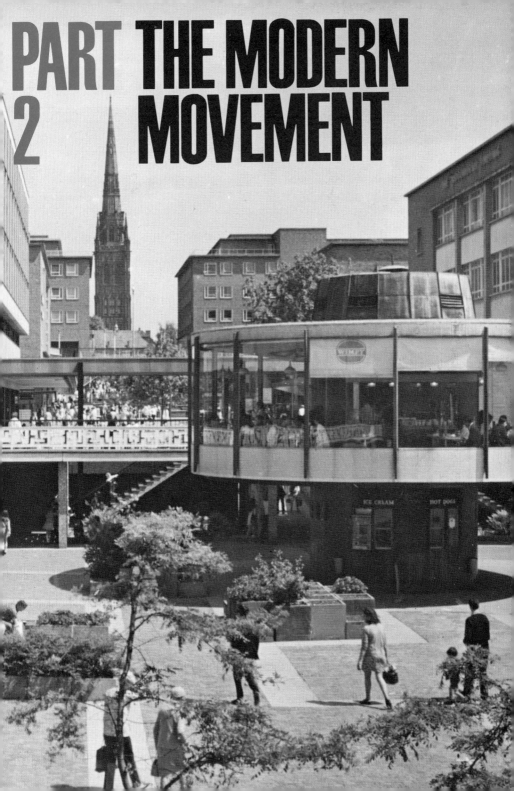

PART 2 THE MODERN MOVEMENT

THE MODERN MOVEMENT
5 A BRIEF REVIEW OF CURRENT TRENDS

Doubts about planning

Despite the considerable achievements of British town planning, the late 1950s saw a growing disillusionment and scepticism. The housing problem persisted; too many redeveloped areas seemed to the public anonymous and lacking in human scale; increased road traffic (see Chapter 9) carried congestion, fumes and danger into shopping and residential streets. For all this the public blamed "the planners".

Yet in truth the system was much at fault. The 1940s plan-making process had proved too inflexible for the rapidly changing 1960s. Instead of the expected static population of 45 million, we had 50 million people by 1951, 55 million by 1965. Increasing prosperity, increasing expectations and multiplication of households all fuelled demand for more and better housing, and increased people's discontent with poor environments. Public opinion increasingly recognised that new buildings alone did not transform cramped lives. In some areas polluted air and water, the squalid surroundings of dereliction and deep-seated social malaise too often persisted (see Chapter 10).

New systems, new attitudes

Appointed to suggest remedies for a creaking planning system, the Planning Advisory Group in 1965 recommended a radical recasting. This reform (see Chapter 6), implemented in 1968, sought to create a flexible plan-making process which would respond to the experience of implementation as well as changing situations and policies. The planner now consciously aims at a moving target.

The Ministry of Housing and Local Government, since 1951 responsible for housing, new towns, public health and local government administration generally, gave way to the even more comprehensive Department of the Environment, which was created by merging the Ministry of Housing and Local Government with the ministries responsible for transport and public buildings. For the first time, one minister [1] – the Secretary of State for the Environment – took responsibility for the whole field of planning and environmental protection, including pollution control. This promised to avert damaging clashes of interest between, for instance, town planners and road planners.

Local authorities – in Britain the primary planning authorities – also changed. In 1965 the GLC and 32 London boroughs superseded more than 80 councils in Greater London's 1,600 sq km. In 1974 a different two-tier system replaced 1,390 councils outside London [2] with 422 – 53 county councils and 369 district councils. Nine regional water authorities are now responsible for water supply, sewage disposal and water pollution control.

Notes
1. The Secretaries of State for Scotland and Wales exercise similar functions in these countries through the Scottish Development Department in Edinburgh and the Welsh Office in Cardiff.
2. In England and Wales. Scottish local government was reorganised in 1975, with a somewhat different two-tier system with nine regions, 53 districts and three islands areas. In Northern Ireland, also in 1975, the number of local authorities was reduced from 78 to 26 and many major services were given to appointed area boards and to departments of the Northern Ireland government.

THE MODERN MOVEMENT

6

THE PLANNING SYSTEM

National planning

Britain has no "national plan" for urban and land development. Central government, however, plans and controls on a national basis capital spending on such projects as schools, hospitals and public housing; and the development of main roads, railways, ports, airports and water resources all goes forward in accordance with national programmes. Central government also closely controls location of industry and employment and the pattern of new town development. It provides much of the data – for instance on population and economic prospects – which form the basis of regional and local planning.

Regional planning

Early regional plans – of which the 1944 Abercrombie Plan for Greater London was an example – did not grapple with social and economic problems. Consequently in 1964 the Government introduced "economic planning councils", appointed from a wide range of interests in each region. The councils work alongside "economic planning boards", composed of top civil servants from the regional offices of such ministries as Employment, Industry and Agriculture and chaired by the Department of the Environment's regional director.

This has facilitated the production of regional strategies, jointly commissioned by central government, the economic planning councils and local planning authorities. These strategies – the first of which, for the south-east, appeared in 1970 – are generally the work of mixed professional teams including town planners, architects, surveyors, economists, engineers, geographers and social scientists. The purpose of the regional strategies is to guide a region's physical, economic and social development.

Structure and local plans

Plan-making at local authority level now (see Chapter 5) follows the pattern prescribed by the 1971 Town and Country Planning Act. County councils prepare "structure plans"; district councils generally prepare "local plans". Structure plans, unlike the old development plans, look not at detailed land-used allocation but at broad policies for physical development, traffic and transport, and improvement of the environment. They look forward over a 15-year period and try to take account of population changes, employment and incomes, availability of resources, housing, industry and commerce, transport, shopping, education, social and community services, recreation and leisure, conservation, and the provision of basic services like water, electricity, gas and sewerage. The "cutting edge" of the structure plan is a programme for the immediate next 10 years, realistic in relation to likely resources. The structure plan is "rolled forward" from one 10-year programme to another in a process of continuous monitoring and modification[1].

Local plans are of three kinds: "action area plans" for "action areas" pinpointed by structure plans as requiring priority development, redevelopment or improvement; "subject plans" on such topics as mineral extraction; and "district plans" to provide a more detailed policy framework for day-to-day planning decisions. In general, local plans are prepared by district councils.

Structure plans need ministerial approval and are first tested by a new form of public inquiry, the "examination in public", at which a panel of people experienced in public affairs hear arguments on selected issues from invited bodies and individuals and report their findings to the Secretary of State. Local plans do not normally need ministerial approval, but must be in accordance with the approved structure plan and can be challenged on specific points by objectors at a public inquiry.

Development control

Within the policy framework provided by local and structure plans, local planning authorities exercise day-to-day planning control over individual sites and applications. Here again the process is flexible: it is not based on any rigid zoning rules. Rather, the authority for the purpose – usually the planning committee of the district council – has discretion to allow good development which fits the spirit if not the letter of the policies it is interpreting. Part of the price for this flexibility may, however, be controversy and delay, especially given the developer's right of appeal to the minister against a planning refusal. A major review in 1975 suggested that the current system of development control was basically sound. Certain minor adjustments were

---

1. In Scotland the structure plan system differs.

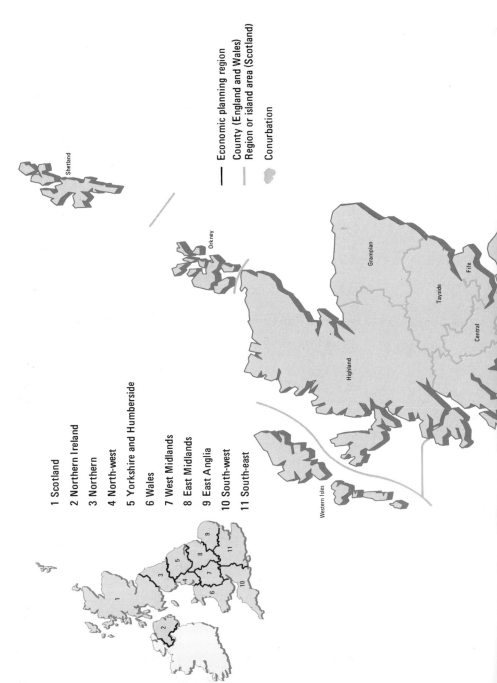

1 Scotland
2 Northern Ireland
3 Northern
4 North-west
5 Yorkshire and Humberside
6 Wales
7 West Midlands
8 East Midlands
9 East Anglia
10 South-west
11 South-east

Economic planning region
County (England and Wales)
Region or island area (Scotland)

Conurbation

Shetland

Orkney

Grampian

Tayside

Fife

Central

Highland

Western Isles

Economic planning regions and main local government areas.

made, particularly to improve the responsiveness of the system to public interest.

Planning and the citizen

Structure plans, local plans and specific planning decisions alike can radically affect the lives of individuals and communities. For that reason, legislation builds into the planning process the citizen's right to participate in plan-making at an early stage, and to be consulted before a decision is taken which may adversely affect him. Local authorities must advertise many classes of planning applications and allow time for comment before reaching a decision; and they are required to indicate to the minister how they have taken the public's views into account in plan-making.

Strengths and shortcomings

The Department of the Environment has phased in the new structure plan/local plan system gradually. As yet we cannot judge how well it will avoid the old pitfalls. In principle, it decentralises real planning power; and indeed ministerial policy is not to modify local decisions except where they conflict with broad national or regional policies. The 1974 local government reorganisation (see Chapter 5) largely divided strategic planning from local planning and implementation. With some shared functions, smooth operation of the system requires high levels of co-operation and compromise between counties and districts, which they have not yet everywhere achieved.

Another weakness in the planning systems stems from land ownership and prices. The present Government believes that only community ownership of major development sites will make possible positive and effective planning in the community's interests (see Chapter 10).

THE MODERN MOVEMENT

7 THE REGIONS AND EMPLOYMENT

Industrial location policies

An aspect of regional planning separate from the preparation of
planning strategies for each region concerns national policies
aimed at correcting economic imbalance *between* regions. From
the 1920s onwards, while the expanding Midlands and south-east
drew new industry, in northern England, Scotland, Wales and
Northern Ireland traditional industry declined, leaving these
regions with unemployment rates often twice the national average.

Successive governments saw this as socially damaging and
economically wasteful, and, following earlier efforts between the
wars, the 1945 Distribution of Industry Act sought to steer
development to places where it would serve the interests of the
whole community and not just the convenience of the industrialist.

It introduced "development areas" chosen by reference to
unemployment rates, and gave government powers to encourage
industrial development on a regional basis. In certain areas,
industrialists need an "industrial development certificate"
from central government for all but quite small factories and
factory extensions.

Regional incentives

Different governments have at different times offered varying
inducements to industry to move to such assisted areas, including
loans, grants, tax allowances; the provision of "advance" [1] and
"bespoke" [2] factories, and in some cases rent-free periods; and
the "regional employment premium" – a direct subsidy per
person employed paid to employers in manufacturing industry.
These policies can show some notable successes, but on the whole
have had less effect on employment rates than movements in the

35

economy generally. The Government has given an undertaking to continue such regional measures at least until 1978 [3].

None the less, policies of upgrading the environment and improving infrastructure in the less favoured regions – for instance, by creating better housing and building motorways – have improved both their quality of life and economic wellbeing. Central government is continuing to invest heavily in regional regeneration and special development agencies have been established in Wales and Scotland to promote industrial revitalisation and environmental improvement. (See also Chapter 11.)

Control of offices

Rapid increases in office employment in central London during the 1950s and 1960s aggravated regional imbalance and caused congestion. The Government set up the Location of Offices Bureau to encourage firms to move out, and in 1964 made planning permission in certain areas subject to central government's granting "office development permits". As the major office employer in London, it is also committed to dispersing its own "headquarters" staffs.

Notes
1. "Advance" factory – factory built by a public agency in advance of a potential user being identified.
2. "Bespoke" factory – factory similarly built but to a prospective user's specification.
3. The European Community's transitional arrangements for British membership end in 1978.

THE MODERN MOVEMENT
8 HOUSING

Aims and needs

Provision of good housing must constitute a major aim of urban planning. People should be well housed at acceptable cost in a good environment reasonably close to their work. In Britain this has been made more difficult by rising demand and a decaying 19th-century housing stock. Population has risen 40 per cent since 1901, but the number of households has doubled. Families are smaller, different generations less ready to share, and there are more one-person households.

Britain has met demand in five main ways: local authority housing for rent on new sites; new town housing for rent (see Chapter 4); new building for sale by private developers; local authority clearance and redevelopment of slums; and improvement and conversion of existing homes [1], by both public and private owners. Additionally, voluntary housing societies, aided by public money, are increasingly providing rented homes for particular groups and needs.

New public housing

Local authority housing for rent ("council housing") on green-field sites, often in large edge-of-town estates, accounted for a large part of the post-war housing drive. In the peak year, 1968, Britain completed 425,000 new homes, about half of them public housing to rent. The Parker Morris Report [2] (1961) set better internal standards, especially as to space and heating.

Housing for sale

Almost all post-war privately built housing has been for sale to owner-occupiers, whose households now account for about half the population. Government policy has encouraged this by tax relief (reducing mortgage interest by one-third) or an equivalent subsidy ("mortgage option") for those with low taxable incomes. Four-fifths of mortgage finance comes from non-profit-making building societies, which normally lend more than £3,000 million a year.

Slum clearance

Slum areas by their nature were usually overcrowded (see Chapter 2), but their inhabitants, low-paid and dependent on local jobs, lacked mobility. Local authorities sought to rehouse as many as possible in the cleared areas; and in the 1960s high-rise blocks

Early post-war schemes to replace unsuitable housing in the older towns made extensive use of high-rise blocks of flats, which seemed to make the best use of limited space. But although many interesting schemes were built, such as those at Roehampton in London (left) and Park Hill in Sheffield (below left), serious social drawbacks were often found, such as the isolation of children from play areas. The emphasis today is on the rehabilitation of existing streets and houses wherever possible, as at Blackburn, Lancashire (above right), and New Earswick, York (below right), or on new low-rise, high-density schemes (see next page).

of flats seemed to offer the easiest and quickest answers. Public opinion later turned against these as a general solution for being inhuman in scale and unsuitable for families with small children; and present policies generally favour carefully planned low-rise, high-density layouts including many individual houses with gardens or patios.

Housing rehabilitation

Government policy in recent years has increasingly encouraged improvement and conversion of sub-standard housing as an alternative to clear-and-rebuild solutions. Rehabilitation gives a double advantage: it preserves the social fabric and makes more economical use of resources, including the skills of small builders. With the help of "improvement grants", allocated by local

Typical recent housing schemes, providing plenty of traffic-free spaces and a community feeling: (this page) Marquess Road, Islington, London; (facing page) winners of Department of the Environment awards to encourage good design in housing – old people's homes at Ashtead, Surrey (top), local authority houses and flats in Lambeth, London (middle), and private flats at Skelton in Cleveland (bottom).

authorities but financed by central government, more than 1.5 million homes have been improved to modern standards since 1949.

Official studies showed, however, that surroundings and not just houses must be upgraded to make them acceptable to residents. So central government introduced "general improvement areas", in which local authorities have power to provide amenities like trees, play areas and car parking, and to divert through traffic. Councils have to date declared more than 1,000 such areas.

But physical improvement of the housing stock was not by itself enough. Grant-aided improvement sometimes led, especially in areas of social stress, to wide-scale displacement of existing tenants by better-off newcomers. Improvement grants were made more selective in 1974, and "housing action areas" were created in which local authorities gained wider powers to intervene and rehabilitate for the benefit of existing inhabitants.

Housing associations

The Government, through its Housing Corporation, is seeking to encourage a variety of voluntary housing associations – non-profit-making bodies providing homes for rent – to help make good a contraction of privately rented housing. The Government provides grant aid, the recently expanded Housing Corporation offers mortgage finance and advice. Local authorities frequently make loans in return for the right to nominate a certain number of tenants. The Government expects housing associations and housing societies (providing co-ownership housing) eventually to contribute 40,000–50,000 extra homes a year.

Britain now has nearly 20 million houses for its 55 million people, 40 per cent built in the last 30 years. But 3 million are sub-standard, and lack of cheap rented housing in stress areas means a growing problem of homelessness. A fundamental review of housing finance is now in progress.

Notes

1. Houses means throughout the book "houses, flats and other self-contained dwellings".
2. Parker Morris Report – the outcome of an inquiry set by the Central Housing Advisory Committee in 1959 to look into standards of design for houses and flats.

THE MODERN MOVEMENT
9 TRANSPORT

Growth of road traffic

Growth of road traffic in the last 20 years has exceeded
expectations. In 1946 there were 2 million private cars; in 1974,
14 million. Economic growth generated more freight, and road
transport generally offered a more convenient, flexible and cheaper
means of moving it from factory to shop. It grew at the expense of
the railways, whose share of total freight fell from 44 per cent in
1953 to 18 per cent 20 years later.

Railway system pruned

The Government brought in Dr (later Lord) Beeching to rescue
railway finances by drastically pruning the network; but the
social costs of abandoning uneconomic branch-lines led to a
system of special subsidies to preserve specific services. The
railways now concentrate on bulk freight, fast "inter-city"
passenger services and commuter services in the conurbations;
and the allocation of capital resources reflects this emphasis.

Traffic in towns

Growth of road traffic showed its sharpest impact in towns.
Sprawling suburbs not easily served by public transport
encouraged car use. Local and central government sought
remedies for congestion in piecemeal improvement, new road
proposals, traffic management and parking controls; but shortage
of funds and public opposition limited what could be done. In
London, with its extensive Underground and rail network, 90 per
cent of journeys to work are still by public transport. Elsewhere,
road congestion crippled bus services and further encouraged car
use, while leaving most people still dependent on deteriorating
public transport.

Buchanan Report

By the early 1960s, concern about the effects of traffic on towns
unable to bear it led to the 1963 Buchanan Report[1], which
pointed out that there were absolute limits to the amount of
traffic towns could accept. Up to these limits, acceptable levels
depended on people's agreement to, and willingness to pay for,
the physical changes involved. Society, said Buchanan, could not
for very long go on spending millions on motor vehicles and
relatively little on roads. One bonus of new urban road systems
would be the creation of largely traffic-free "environmental areas"
in residential and shopping zones. The report urged that land-use
and transport must be planned together.

Motorways and trunk roads.

Motorways in use or nearing completion

Other trunk roads
(dual carriageways shown heavier)

Conurbations

The huge growth in road transport since the war has been met by the building of motorways linking the main cities and by the extensive improvement of other roads. Where possible through traffic is made to bypass towns or is restricted to special routes. In addition, streets in many older town centres have been fully pedestrianised, as in Norwich, Norfolk (above), and Leeds, West Yorkshire (right).

Problems of urban roads

For the rest of the 1960s, this principle guided transport planning; a series of land-use/transportation studies for London and other towns brought traffic considerations into the centre of land-use planning. Local authorities embarked with central government grant-aid on ambitious urban motorway projects, often with scant regard for their environmental and social impact. By 1970 public opposition to urban motorways became a powerful political force; many people suspected that new, high-capacity urban roads, far from relieving congestion, often worsened it by attracting extra traffic. The report of the Urban Motorways Committee in 1972 identified traffic noise, severance of communities, visual intrusion and disturbance during construction as major problems, and suggested ways in which road-planners could avoid or mitigate them. Its report also led to legislation which requires highway authorities to sound-proof houses affected by new roads and in certain cases pay cash compensation to house-owners. Shortage of funds and changing public attitudes have since cut urban road building to a minimum.

Transport planning has more recently concentrated on measures to restrain private car use and parking and to assist public transport. Local authorities largely decide the nature and extent of such measures, within the limits set by transport policies and programmes, comprehensive spending proposals which county councils make annually to the Department of the Environment and which form the basis of central government's allocations of grant aid. In large conurbations, special passenger transport executives, responsible to metropolitan county councils, co-ordinate and promote bus and rail services.

New solutions

With growing financial stringency, the amounts available for ambitious public transport projects, as for roads, have disappointed the counties. Two conurbations, Merseyside and Tyneside, are, however, pressing ahead with important multi-million-pound rapid-transit projects. The general approach to urban traffic problems has moved from major surgery to a conservationist, incremental approach. Cities more and more see traffic-free zones as the answer to dangerous and congested conditions in central shopping areas. Leeds now enjoys 900 metres of shopping streets free of all but delivery traffic; Nottingham is experimenting with computerised traffic restraint and bus priority measures. New roads in towns now generally take the form of modest diversions and improvements, not major motorways.

The inter-urban motorway and trunk road programme continues, though more slowly. By 1974 the length of motorway and high-

Some towns have ambitious public transport schemes, such as the advanced tramway system being built for the Tyneside conurbation (right) and the special Busway in Runcorn New Town (below right).

quality (semi-motorway) dual carriageway totalled 3,875 km[2].
The programme gives high priority to local bypasses which take
traffic out of narrow congested high streets. The economics of
scale, aided by "containerisation", have encouraged use of larger
and larger lorries, which cause considerable environmental
problems. Current proposals to canalise lorry traffic onto a limited
set of special lorry routes may help, but provoke controversy
because in many areas – particularly in London – all existing
routes have their environmental drawbacks.

Notes

1. Sir Colin Buchanan b. 1907, land-use and transport planner, led the team which
produced *Traffic in Towns*; later founded a consultancy which has produced many plans
and studies for towns in Britain and overseas.
2. Excluding Northern Ireland.

London has a very large and well-patronised public transport system, including the extensive Underground (left), although some suburban areas are not suitable for the provision of full services, which has led to the introduction of "mini" buses (right), while in the crowded central area buses have to compete for road space with private and commercial traffic, so that bus-only lanes have been introduced where possible (below).

49

THE MODERN MOVEMENT

10 PROBLEMS IN URBAN DEVELOPMENT

Pressures on land

Land for development, a very scarce resource in Britain, came under strong pressure during the 1960s and 1970s as a growing population and higher expectations fuelled demand for more houses, schools, hospitals, factories, shops, roads and recreational open space. The development plan system seeks to allocate available land to best advantage. But actual development depends on someone buying the land and obtaining planning consent for a particular project.

Land values and development

Public authorities seeking land for such purposes as municipal housing, roads or town centre redevelopment can, in default of agreement, use powers of compulsory purchase. Such compulsory purchase orders require ministerial approval and are subject to public inquiry; the price paid is current market price. But much development remains in private hands, and the price paid depends on market forces. The grant of planning permission normally raises its value considerably; the prospect of development or redevelopment has tended to inflate land values in and around towns, often quite rapidly.

The present Government's policy is that community ownership of all but minor development land will alone provide "a real system of planning that has as its basis the needs of the community and not the demands of the market place" [1]. Legislation gives local authorities [2] wide powers to buy land for private development; and ultimately envisages a duty to acquire virtually all land needed for private development of any real size for up to 10 years ahead. Initially, sellers of development land will pay an 80 per cent tax on the enhancement element of the land's value, and local authorities can deduct this from the price they pay; later they will be able to buy land at current use value, excluding its development potential. They can later sell back to developers at current market value.

Social planning
Improvement of social conditions has long been a prime goal of planning, but the scale and speed of change in recent decades have thrown into relief its social effects and implications. Planners came to realise that large-scale urban renewal intended to give people better homes might seriously damage the "root systems" of established communities.

The 1968 reorganisation of local authorities' social services enabled directors of the unified departments to advise on social considerations affecting planning; and the improved information thus available has encouraged planners to take a much wider account of social factors than hitherto.

The inner city
Perhaps the most intractable problem of recent years concerns the run-down inner areas of large cities, where physical, economic and social handicaps reinforce each other to produce a cycle of deprivation. Poor housing and poor general environment lead to low rents, which in turn attract predominantly the poorly paid and unskilled – including many immigrants. Planning policy has encouraged industry to move from these areas, thus curtailing employment opportunities. Low incomes from the relatively poorly paid service jobs make it difficult for them to move away. Demolition and decay stamp such areas with an environmental "mark of Cain"; vandalism and crime increase; and local authorities feel constrained to spend most of their limited funds elsewhere in areas of growing population and demands.

Causes of decline
Central government has tried to tackle these problems. A series of "community development projects" [3] has sought to identify the causes of deprivation and the needs of individual communities. They have confirmed beyond doubt that the inner city's decline results from an external economic process, not from any change in the behaviour pattern of the inhabitants.

Help for stress areas
The Home Office's Urban Programme has sought to supplement with limited funds (£55m–£70m over eight years) the efforts of the major programmes by providing quickly in stress areas extra facilities not otherwise available, such as day nurseries, nursery schools, and old people's lunch clubs and day centres. It has also established a special Urban Deprivation Unit to make further studies; and studies commissioned by the Department of the Environment into specific inner city districts are working on

The best new developments have considered the individual needs of all who live in them, including the old and the disabled.

Community health and welfare:
(Left) Old people's flats form part of this housing scheme at Marquess Road, Islington, London.
(Above) Lakeside Health Centre at Thamesmead, a large riverside development in south-east London that will eventually house 60,000 people.
(Above right) One of a series of bungalows, set in large grounds, forming a community for mentally handicapped children at Westoning, Bedfordshire.
(Right) A health centre at Wellingborough, Northamptonshire, commissioned by five major medical practices in the town to pool their resources and enable them to improve their services.

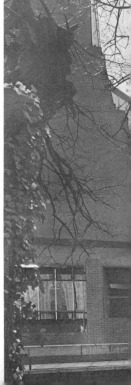

Education:
(Top) Nursery school
at Milton Keynes,
Buckinghamshire.
(Above) Gymnasium at
Pimlico Comprehensive
School, London.
(Above right) The
University of Stirling,
Scotland, with 3,009
students, is set in an
18th-century park.

(Right) The Florey
Building, a hall of
residence for students at
Queen's College,
Oxford.

Civic amenities:
(Left) The Haymarket
Theatre at Leicester.
(Below) A public
library at Maidenhead,
Berkshire.
(Right) Traffic-free
shopping area at
Camberley, Surrey.
(Below right) Large
covered shopping
concourse at Runcorn
New Town.

Modern town centres are designed primarily for the convenience of those working and shopping there, with extensive pedestrianised areas and convenient but separate parking places. (Left) In Blackburn, Lancashire, the local authority offices form part of a complex with shopping.

proposals for reversing their decline. Some local authorities now have special units to co-ordinate services at a neighbourhood level, with local representative groups participating in management.

Destruction of town centres by wartime bombing gave some local authorities the chance to rebuild more attractively and efficiently. Coventry stands out as an instance of the imaginative use of such opportunities. Slum clearance also provided scope for large-scale rebuilding; and the growing prosperity of the 1960s attracted commercial and property companies to invest private capital in town centre rebuilding, with large new blocks of offices and shops. Often achieved by a partnership of local authority and commercial developer, the better schemes achieved good design standards as well as providing traffic-free shopping and segregated goods delivery.

Notes

1. The Minister for Planning and Local Government, Mr John Silkin, commending the Bill to the House of Commons on 29 April 1975.
2. In Wales, special land authorities will exercise these functions.
3. Community development project-action research into the social needs of a small local community including central and local government, voluntary groups and the local community themselves.

Factories and offices:
(Top) The Olivetti
factory at Tadworth,
Surrey.
(Middle) Efficient use of
valuable space in an
office in the Greater
London Council's
extension block, itself
built on a previously
undeveloped site in the
centre of a large road
intersection near
Westminster Bridge.
(Bottom) A new building
in the centre of
Ipswich, Suffolk, for an
insurance company
moving its operations
from London.

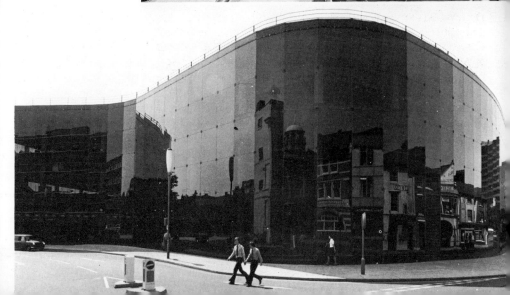

11

SAFEGUARDING THE COUNTRY'S HERITAGE

Growth of conservation

Britain has a rich urban heritage, long under-valued and neglected. Dissatisfaction with much new development has, however, quickened a growing appreciation. At first voluntary bodies were the main preservers – outstandingly the National Trust which, founded in 1895, now cares for over 200 historic buildings. Government first became involved with protection of ancient monuments, but has increasingly intervened to safeguard historic buildings and areas. It has now listed over 200,000 buildings of special architectural or historic importance, which no one may demolish without official permission. Local authorities and preservation societies have increasingly bought, repaired, or aided the repair of historic buildings.

Buildings in context

The Civic Trust has promoted "face-lifts" to brighten drab or untidy streets, and educated public opinion with its annual awards for buildings and urban improvements. It particularly stressed the need to conserve and enhance the overall urban scene rather than just outstanding individual buildings; and in 1967 local authorities were given power to designate conservation areas[1], of which there are now more than 3,000, and in which any demolition now requires planning consent.

Pollution control

The Alkali Inspectorate, founded in 1863, was probably the world's first air pollution control agency. Its continuing efforts

There are numerous bodies, many of them voluntary, that concern themselves with the care of the country's heritage. The Civic Trust gives annual awards for outstanding examples of the protection or improvement of individual buildings or whole areas. These two schemes won awards in 1975:
(Top right) Preservation of the Guildhall, Poole, Dorset, and its surrounding area.
(Right) Rehabilitation of nine derelict houses in Lambeth, London, dating from about 1820, to provide new homes.

were supplemented in 1956 and 1968 by Acts which have made 7 million homes and commercial premises subject to smoke control and, despite a 17 per cent increase in energy consumption, reduced domestic smoke by two-thirds. In 1951 a period began of co-operative endeavours by dischargers of effluent and authorities to reduce water pollution. In the period 1958–72 they reduced the length of grossly polluted waterways from 2,588 km to 1,833 km. Fish are returning to waters where they have not been seen in this century. In noise pollution, transport is the main offender. British measures, like those of other countries, concentrate on ensuring quieter aircraft and road vehicles. (But see Chapter 9.)

Rural population policies

Though much of Britain is urbanised and industrial, three-quarters of its land surface is used for agriculture and one-fifth of its people live in rural areas. But of these only a fifth work on the land [2]. The wish of commuters and retired people to live in the country has kept rural populations high in some areas; but in remote and upland districts, a poor choice of jobs causes young people to migrate, giving rise to problems of depopulation. Planning policies and selective government aid seek to control these trends and stimulate employment.

Countryside conservation

Whether we regard the countryside as a source of food (it supplies half Britain's needs), scenic heritage or wildlife habitat, urban expansion puts it under increasing pressure. The townsman demands land for houses, roads and reservoirs and access for recreation, and new farming methods themselves radically alter some landscapes. In seeking to reconcile these conflicting interests, the Government has the advice of the Countryside Commission for England and Wales, the Countryside Commission for Scotland, and the Nature Conservancy Council [3]. National policy severely restricts development in open country and outside key settlements, and helps to protect sensitive areas by the designation of national parks, areas of outstanding natural beauty, nature reserves (140 in England and Wales) and sites of special scientific interest [4] (over 3,000) which contain rare flora and fauna.

National parks, recreation and conservation

Following recommendations of the Scott Committee (see Chapter 3), the 1949 National Parks and Access to the Countryside Act established a National Parks Commission. This body (now the Countryside Commission) designates national parks in England and Wales [4], seeking to protect their natural beauty and encourage within them open-air recreation and the study of nature. Introducing the Bill, the minister called it "a people's charter for the open air, for hikers and ramblers, for everyone who lives in a town to get out into the open air and enjoy the countryside".

Since then ministers have confirmed the designation of 10 national parks (including the Lake District, Snowdonia and the Peak District) covering in all 13,618 sq km, or 9 per cent of the land area of England and Wales. Designation involves no change in ownership; its aim is to conserve fine natural landscape and provide better public access and enjoyment without interference with agriculture. Each park has its own national park authority, which is responsible for managing recreational demands on the parks, exercises most planning functions within it, and receives substantial grant aid from central government. The Commission also designates areas of outstanding natural beauty and promotes country parks and other informal recreational facilities. Local authorities have, in the 27 years since the Act was passed, completed surveys of all public footpaths; they and the Commission have established several long-distance footpaths, including the 400-km Pennine Way and many coastal footpaths.

Recreational pressure from heavily populated urban areas poses one of the biggest threats to rural conservation, and the mobility of a car-using population potentially threatens the very peace and beauty people travel to find. National policy seeks to reconcile this basic conflict by careful planning and management – guiding leisure journeys to the areas that can absorb them, providing special attractions with adequate space for cars, such as country parks and picnic sites, and in the last resort restraining traffic flows. Countryside "interpretation" – schemes to reveal and explain the countryside to townspeople – offers another means of preventing damaging conflict.

Green belts
The 1944 Abercrombie plan for Greater London proposed a green belt round London extending some 15–20 km beyond the built-up area. The Government accepted this, and local planning authorities have stringently maintained it, refusing development which would erode it both from the edge of built-up London and from towns within the belt. In 1955 the minister asked authorities to propose green belts round other towns and conurbations, to check urban sprawl, prevent neighbouring towns from merging, and preserve the character of certain towns.

Coastal heritage
Britain enjoys a long and often beautiful coastline for its size. National Trust ownership and "heritage coast" designation in county structure plans afford considerable protection to the finest, unspoiled stretches. Exceptionally, economic arguments override conservation: for instance, the development needs of North Sea oil – to service exploration rigs, build production platforms and land oil and gas – are making a major impact on remote and hitherto unspoiled coastal areas in Scotland. Public opinion broadly accepts this price and the Scottish Development

Preservation of the countryside:
(Right) The boating lake in the Goyt Valley, in the Peak District National Park, Derbyshire; a minibus service runs from a car park at the head of the valley, keeping cars from the lakeside itself. (Below right) Highway engineers, faced with the problem of taking a motorway through the narrow Lune Gorge, Cumbria, without spoiling its beauty, built the road close to the contours of the land.

Two scenes in Snowdonia National Park, Wales: pony-trekking near Cader Idris and a view of Pen-yr-oleu-wen.

Green belts, national parks and areas of outstanding natural beauty.

National parks
(in Scotland national park direction areas)

Areas of outstanding natural beauty

Green belts

National forest parks

Long-distance footpaths

Conurbations

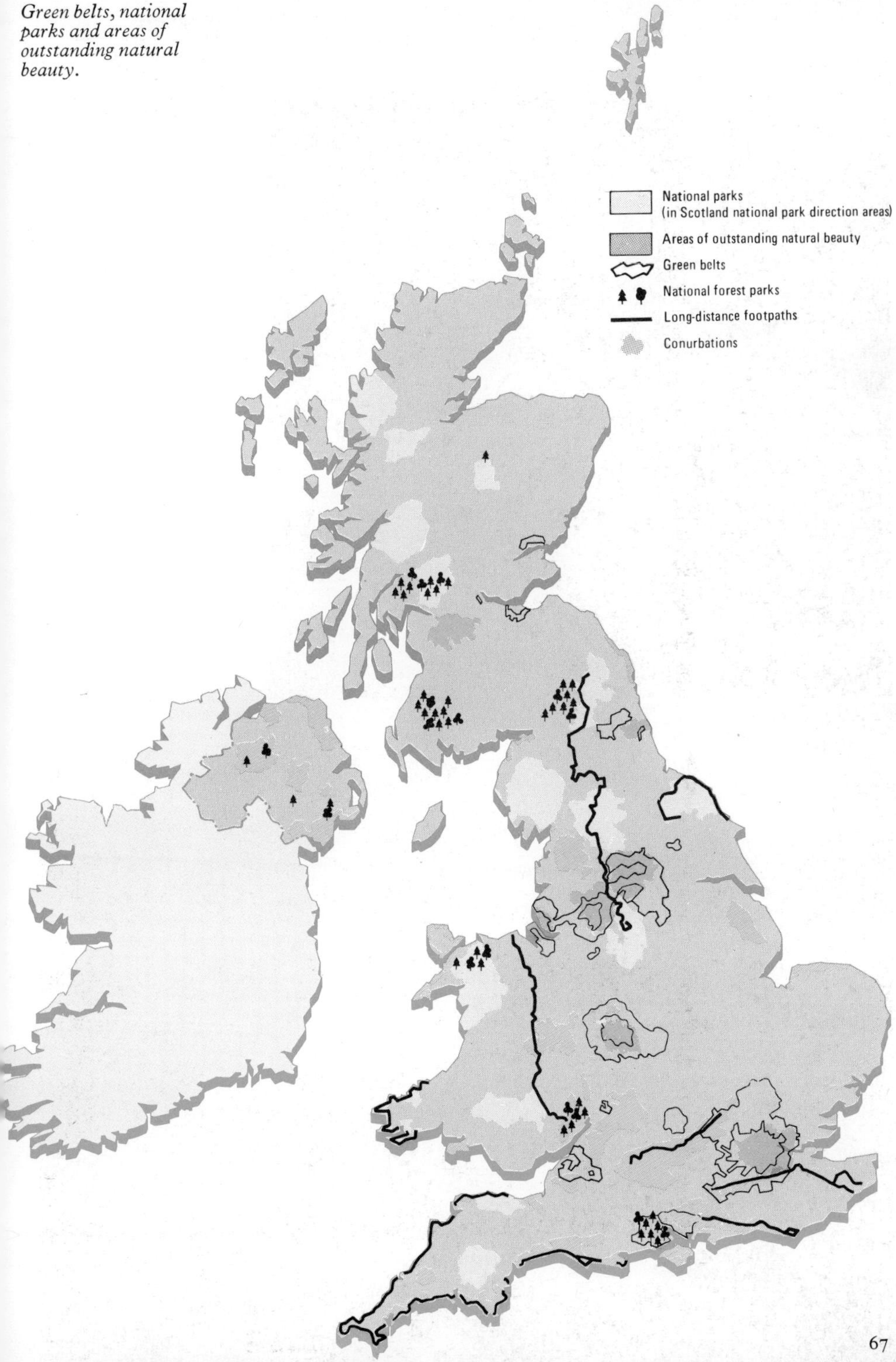

Wherever possible, lakes and waterways are preserved – or created – for recreation:
(Left) These "narrow boats", originally used to carry goods on Britain's extensive canal system, have been converted into pleasure boats for holidaymakers.
(Right) The Lakeland Marina, near Kesh, Fermanagh, Northern Ireland.
(Below right) Disused gravel workings at Holme Pierrepont, Nottinghamshire, have been converted into an international rowing centre – the 1975 world championships were held there.

Department has prepared "coastal planning guidelines" which seek to mitigate the damage.

Land reclamation

Many urban and rural areas are disfigured by industrial dereliction, the total area of which a 1974 survey put at some 54,000 hectares. Owners and operators owed no legal duty to restore past dereliction, so that central government offered local authorities grants ranging from 50 per cent to 85 per cent to undertake this work. It now proposes to raise grant rates in England's worst areas to 100 per cent and to establish special agencies to tackle reclamation in Wales and Scotland. Planning authorities now normally make restoration programmes a condition of consent.

Notes

1. Conservation area – a selected group of buildings or area marked out by a local authority to be conserved and enhanced as a group. The designation does not prevent sympathetic redevelopment of individual sites, but ensures that any proposals for change are carefully scrutinised.
2. That is, employed in agriculture, forestry, fishing and mineral extraction.
3. In Northern Ireland, official conservation bodies include the Ulster Countryside Committee and the Nature Reserves Committee.
4. Sites of special scientific interest – designated by the Nature Conservancy Council – are areas chosen either because of their wildlife communities (plants, animals) or special geological features.

APPRAISAL

Humility needed

This short book does not of course tell the complete story. British experience springs from more than a century of pioneering efforts to plan for a better human habitat: but many grave problems remain and many a confidently propounded solution has spawned new problems. Which all suggests that wise urban planning demands a delicate balance of courage, imagination and humility.

Planning – by public demand

One lesson few people in Britain question: that planning is needed. Our bitter past experience cannot be denied: the free play of market forces does not produce a good environment. Yet the growth of planning control has been evolutionary. Each extension of control has been by public demand, to remedy a proven malaise – urban sprawl, economic imbalance, unacceptable traffic growth and unsightly mineral extraction are just four examples.

A constant dialogue

Another lesson to be drawn is the need for a constant dialogue between planners and implementers of development. Planning needs to establish a continuing rapport, both with developers – or it will prove sterile – and the public – or it may court damaging opposition and delay. The days when the "experts" prepared the "right plan", and then explained to the public why it was necessary, have long passed in Britain. Planning now consists in recognising, balancing and adjudicating between complex conflicting interests. It must reconcile "grass-roots" local demands with the overall regional or national needs. Britain works by a series of national policies rather than a single national plan. Planners appreciate the need to make planning more comprehensive, but this is difficult and calls for the continuous attention which it is now being given.

Planning broadly defined
British planning has, however, broadened in two important ways. It has moved away from narrow land-use allocation to serving the community's economic and social goals; and it has become a less finite, more continuous and flexible apparatus. Planning must be able to respond to changing conditions and goals.

Technology's limitations
Another mirage British planners have learned to mistrust is over-reliance on sophisticated techniques, such as mathematical modelling and cost/benefit analysis. In quantifying complex factors, these tools have great value. But they are only tools; their answers are only as good as the information fed into them.

Conserving our habitat
The onset of a period of new economic stringency has also affected British urban planning, according in some ways well with increasingly accepted conservationist doctrines. There is less money for new roads, houses, towns, shopping centres and workplaces, so we must make better use of what we have. Britain today displays an increasing concern to make more careful use of scarce raw materials and other non-renewable resources – none more so than the precious human heritage, slowly and painstakingly evolved, of cities, towns and villages and the man-made landscape which complements them. These are our habitat. We must plan to conserve and enhance them.

Acknowledgments

The illustrations in this book have been reproduced by permission of the individuals and organisations listed below (numbered by pages, with letters indicating position reading down the page):

Front cover Brecht-Einzig Ltd
Inside front cover John Donat/Crown Copyright
6 Central Library, Welwyn Garden City
8 a, b Mansell Collection
10 a, b Mansell Collection
11 a From *The capital of Scotland* by Moray McLaren, Douglas and Foulis, Edinburgh, 1950
b From *Metropolitan improvements* by J Elmes, London, 1827
12 Mansell Collection
14 a, b Aerofilms Ltd
15 City of Liverpool Housing Department
20 a Terry Moore/Welwyn Garden City
b Harlow Development Corporation
21 a, c Crown Copyright
b Harlow Development Corporation
22 a, b Borough of Thamesdown
23 Cumbernauld Development Corporation
24 John Donat/Milton Keynes Development Corporation
25 John Mills/Runcorn Development Corporation
26 Coventry City Council
38 a, b Aerofilms Ltd
39 a, b Crown Copyright
40 a Brecht-Einzig Ltd
b Sam Lambert
c Kershaw Studios, York
41 The Architectural Review
45 a Norwich City Council
b Crown Copyright
47 a Metro-Cammell Ltd
b John Mills/Runcorn Development Corporation
48 London Transport Executive
49 a London Transport Executive
b Fox Photos
52 The Architectural Press
53 a, c Brecht-Einzig Ltd
b MacCormac and Jamieson
54 a John Donat/Milton Keynes Development Corporation
b Brecht-Einzig Ltd
55 a The Architectural Review
b Brecht-Einzig Ltd
56 a, b John Donat
57 a The Architectural Press
b Runcorn Development Corporation
58 Building Design Partnership
59 a, b Brecht-Einzig Ltd
c The Architects' Journal
61 a Sam Lambert/Civic Trust
b Greater London Council/Civic Trust
62 a Aerofilms Ltd
b Derek Pratt/Civic Trust
65 a Peak Park Planning
b John Laing and Son
66 a British Tourist Authority
b E Emrys Jones, Old Colwyn
68 John Donat/Milton Keynes Development Corporation
69 a Northern Ireland Information Service
b Christopher Blackwall
Inside back cover John Donat/Crown Copyright
Back cover Scottish Tourist Board
Special maps and diagrams by Diagram Visual Information Ltd

Recreation in town and country:
(Right) This canal running through the new town of Milton Keynes, Buckinghamshire, provides a pleasant leisure amenity. The picture on the back cover shows climbers in Inverness-shire, Scotland.

Prepared by the Department of the Environment and the Central Office of Information, 1976

Printed for Her Majesty's Stationery Office by Colibri Press Ltd. Dd 290271 3/76 Pro. 6142

© Crown Copyright 1976
First published 1976

Her Majesty's
Stationery Office

Government Bookshops
49 High Holborn
London WC1V 6HB
13a Castle Street
Edinburgh EH2 3AR
41 The Hayes
Cardiff CF1 1JW
Brazennose Street
Manchester M60 8AS
Southey House
Wine Street
Bristol BS1 2BQ
258 Broad Street
Birmingham B1 2HE
80 Chichester Street
Belfast BT1 4JY

Government publications are also available through booksellers